DATE DUE

D0688181

HIGHSMITH #45114

WITHDRAWN

MY FIRST SPORTS

Fishing

by Derek Zobel

BELLWETHER MEDIA · MINNEAPOLIS, MN

Note to Librarians, Teachers, and Parents:

Blastoff! Readers are carefully developed by literacy experts and combine standards-based content with developmentally appropriate text.

Level 1 provides the most support through repetition of high-frequency words, light text, predictable sentence patterns, and strong visual support.

Level 2 offers early readers a bit more challenge through varied simple sentences, increased text load, and less repetition of high-frequency words.

Level 3 advances early-fluent readers toward fluency through increased text and concept load, less reliance on visuals, longer sentences, and more literary language.

Level 4 builds reading stamina by providing more text per page, increased use of punctuation, greater variation in sentence patterns, and increasingly challenging vocabulary.

Level 5 encourages children to move from "learning to read" to "reading to learn" by providing even more text, varied writing styles, and less familiar topics.

Whichever book is right for your reader, Blastoff! Readers are the perfect books to build confidence and encourage a love of reading that will last a lifetime!

This edition first published in 2011 by Bellwether Media, Inc.

No part of this publication may be reproduced in whole or in part without written permission of the publisher. For information regarding permission, write to Bellwether Media, Inc., Attention: Permissions Department, 5357 Penn Avenue South, Minneapolis, MN 55419.

Library of Congress Cataloging-in-Publication Data
Zobel, Derek, 1983–
Fishing / by Derek Zobel.
   p. cm. – (Blastoff! readers : my first sports)
Includes bibliographical references and index.
Summary: "Simple text and full-color photographs introduce beginning readers to the sport of fishing. Developed by literacy experts for students in grades two through five"–Provided by publisher.
   ISBN 978-1-60014-569-8 (hardcover : alk. paper)
1. Fishing–Juvenile literature. I. Title.
SH445.Z63 2010
799.1–dc22   2010035269

Text copyright © 2011 by Bellwether Media, Inc. BLASTOFF! READERS and associated logos are trademarks and/or registered trademarks of Bellwether Media, Inc.

Printed in the United States of America, North Mankato, MN.
010111   1176

Contents

What Is Fishing?

Fishing is an outdoor activity where people catch fish for food, money, or fun. For thousands of years, people have been fishing in rivers, lakes, and oceans.

Ancient peoples fished for survival. They used nets, spears, and even their bare hands to capture fish. They cooked and ate the fish they caught.

In the 1600s and 1700s, people started fishing for fun. This is called **sport fishing**. Today, millions of people around the world enjoy this activity. Fishermen try to catch a variety of **game fish**. They love the thrill of reeling in bass, pikes, and sunfish.

World-Record Game Fish

Fish	Size	Where & When
Black Crappie	4.98 pounds (2.26 kilograms)	Private Lake, Missouri (2006)
Largemouth Bass	22.31 pounds (10.12 kilograms)	Montgomery Lake, Georgia (1932) and Lake Biwa, Japan (2009) (Tie)
Northern Pike	55.12 pounds (25 kilograms)	Lake of Grefeern, Germany (1986)
Walleye	25 pounds (11.34 kilograms)	Old Hickory Lake, Tennessee (1960)
Yellow Perch	4.21 pounds (1.91 kilograms)	Bordentown, New Jersey (1865)

! fun fact

People who fish for sport must buy fishing licenses. A fishing license allows a fisherman to catch certain kinds of fish for a set number of days.

Fishing Styles and Equipment

People use different pieces of equipment for different kinds of fishing. Most people use a **fishing rod** and a **fishing reel**.

The reel holds the fishing line, which is then threaded through the **guides** of the fishing rod. Fishing line is thin, but it is very tough. Some kinds of line can support fish that weigh up to 1,000 pounds (454 kilograms)!

guides

fishing rod

fishing reel

People who use rods and reels can attract fish two different ways. They can use **bobbers** and **live bait**, or they can use **lures**.

lure

bobber

live bait

Both require fishermen to **cast** out their lines.
Fish will try to grab live bait such as worms
and leeches. They will chase after lures that
move underwater the way frogs and fish do.

A bobber attaches to the fishing line. It sits above the end of the line where the hook with the live bait hangs. The bobber floats on the surface of the water, and the hook lies at a **depth** that the fisherman chooses.

When a fish bites, the bobber goes underwater. The fisherman must **set the hook** and turn the reel to bring in the line and the fish!

fun fact
In the winter when lakes freeze, people cut holes in the ice so they can reach the fish below! This is called ice fishing.

fun fact

In large bodies of water, many people enjoy deep-sea fishing. They use huge rods and reels to catch marlins, swordfish, and even sharks!

Lures come in a variety of shapes, sizes, and colors. Sharp hooks are attached to them. Fishermen tie their lures to the end of their lines.

After casting out, a fisherman lets the lure sink a little and then begins reeling in slowly. This makes the lure look like it is swimming, which attracts fish. When a fish bites, the fisherman sets the hook and reels it in.

Every fisherman carries a **tackle box**. This box holds lures, bobbers, hooks, and other fishing equipment.

Fishermen who fish on boats often wear life jackets. Some use **depth finders** to check the depth of the water.

tackle box

Fishing Today

Today, fishing is popular all around the world. Some fishermen practice **catch and release**. After they catch a fish, they put it back into the water.

fun fact

Some fishermen fly-fish in rivers and streams. They let their lines out slowly and move their rods back and forth to drag fake flies across the water.

Other fishermen like to eat the fish they catch. They catch game fish and **fillet** them to eat.

The best fishermen compete in tournaments alone and in teams. Fishermen have a set amount of time to catch the largest game fish they can. The fisherman or fishing team with the heaviest fish reels in the grand prize.

Fishing is an activity that can be enjoyed by people of all ages. With the right practice, equipment, and patience, anyone can be a champion fisherman!

Glossary

bobbers—pieces of fishing equipment that float on the surface of the water; bobbers go underwater when fish bite the live bait on the hooks.

cast—to move a fishing rod in a throwing motion to release fishing line with live bait or a lure

catch and release—a practice where fishermen release the fish that they catch

depth—the measurement of how far something is underwater; fishermen can set the depth at which their bait will lie.

depth finders—electronic devices that show fisherman the depth of the water

fillet—to cut the meat off a fish and prepare it to be cooked

fishing reel—the piece of fishing equipment that holds the fishing line; line comes out of the reel when a fisherman casts out and comes back when a fisherman reels in.

fishing rod—the pole a fisherman holds that guides the line out of the fishing reel

game fish—fish caught for sport; pikes, trout, bass, walleye, and sunfish are examples of game fish.

guides—loops on a fishing rod through which fishing line is threaded

live bait—bait that a fisherman puts on a hook in order to attract fish; worms and leeches are commonly used as live bait.

lures—shiny, colorful pieces of fishing equipment that fishermen use to attract fish; lures have hooks to catch fish.

set the hook—to pull the fishing rod up quickly, which pulls the hook up to catch the fish

sport fishing—fishing for sport; millions of people around the world try to catch fish for fun.

tackle box—the piece of fishing equipment where bobbers, lures, and hooks are stored

To Learn More

AT THE LIBRARY
McMillan, Bruce. *Going Fishing*. Boston, Mass.:
Houghton Mifflin Co., 2005.

Newman, Gary. *Fishing*. New York, N.Y.: Crabtree
Pub., 2009.

Prosek, James. *A Good Day's Fishing*. New York,
N.Y.: Simon & Schuster Books for Young Readers,
2004.

ON THE WEB
Learning more about fishing
is as easy as 1, 2, 3.

1. Go to www.factsurfer.com.

2. Enter "fishing" into the search box.

3. Click the "Surf" button and you will see a list of
   related Web sites.

With factsurfer.com, finding more information is just a
click away.

Index

The images in this book are reproduced through the courtesy of: Andersen Ross/Getty Images, front cover, p. 8; S.M., front cover (small), p. 11 (middle); Sean Boggs, pp. 4-5; North Wind Picture Archives/Alamy, p. 5 (small); Jeff Schultz/Alaskastock/Photolibrary, p. 6; Juan Martinez, p. 7; Brand X Pictures/Photolibrary, p. 9; Michael C. Gray, pp. 10-11; Fedor Kondratenko, p. 11 (top); fotosav, p. 11 (bottom); J. Lethal, pp. 12, 13; imagebroker/Alamy, p. 14; Bill Lindner/Windigo Images, p. 15; ARENA Creative, p. 16 (small); Mark Kayser/Windigo Images, pp. 16-17; Corey Hochachka/Design Pics Inc./Photolibrary, pp. 18-19; Mitch Kezar/Windigo Images, p. 20; Soc Clay/Windigo Images, p. 21.

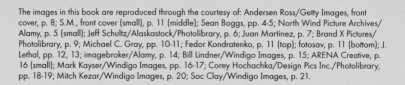